1116

DK

D0459201

PEYTON MANNING

Awesome Athletes

Jameson Anderson

Checkerboard
Library

An Imprint of Abdo Publishing
www.abdopublishing.com

www.abdopublishing.com

Published by Abdo Publishing, a division of ABDO, PO Box 398166, Minneapolis, Minnesota
55439. Copyright © 2015 by Abdo Consulting Group, Inc. International copyrights reserved in all
countries. No part of this book may be reproduced in any form without written permission from
the publisher. Checkerboard Library™ is a trademark and logo of Abdo Publishing.

Printed in the United States of America, North Mankato, Minnesota.
052014
092014

THIS BOOK CONTAINS
RECYCLED MATERIALS

Cover Photo: AP Images
Interior Photos: AP Images pp. 1, 9, 11, 13, 19, 23, 25, 27, 29; Corbis p. 17;
    Getty Images pp. 5, 7, 15, 20

Series Coordinator: Tamara L. Britton
Editor: Rochelle Baltzer
Art Direction: Neil Klinepier

Library of Congress Cataloging-in-Publication Data

Anderson, Jameson.
  Peyton Manning / Jameson Anderson.
    pages cm. -- (Awesome athletes)
  Includes index.
  ISBN 978-1-62403-332-2
1. Manning, Peyton--Juvenile literature. 2. Football players--United States--Biography--Juvenile
literature. I. Title.
  GV939.M289A64 2015
  796.332092--dc23
  [B]
                              2014007149

TABLE OF CONTENTS

Super Bowl Champion 4

Highlight Reel 6

Football Family 8

Prep Star 10

College Days 12

Draft Day. 14

Giving Back. 16

The Colts 18

Injured 22

Comeback 24

Still a Star 26

Lasting Legacy 28

Glossary 30

Websites. 31

Index 32

SUPER BOWL CHAMPION

On February 4, 2007, at Dolphins Stadium in Miami, Florida, Peyton Manning stood at the center of the field. He had just reached a goal he had been working toward his whole life. Manning had led the Indianapolis Colts to a 29–17 win over the Chicago Bears. He was a **Super Bowl** champion.

After the game, reporters and photographers from around the country surrounded Manning. As he hugged teammates and shook hands with members of the Bears, a smile never left his face. After nine years in the **National Football League (NFL)**, he had finally won a Super Bowl.

Some reporters and fans thought that Manning could never win the big game. But Manning proved his critics wrong. In fact, he was named the game's Most Valuable Player (MVP). Could he do it again?

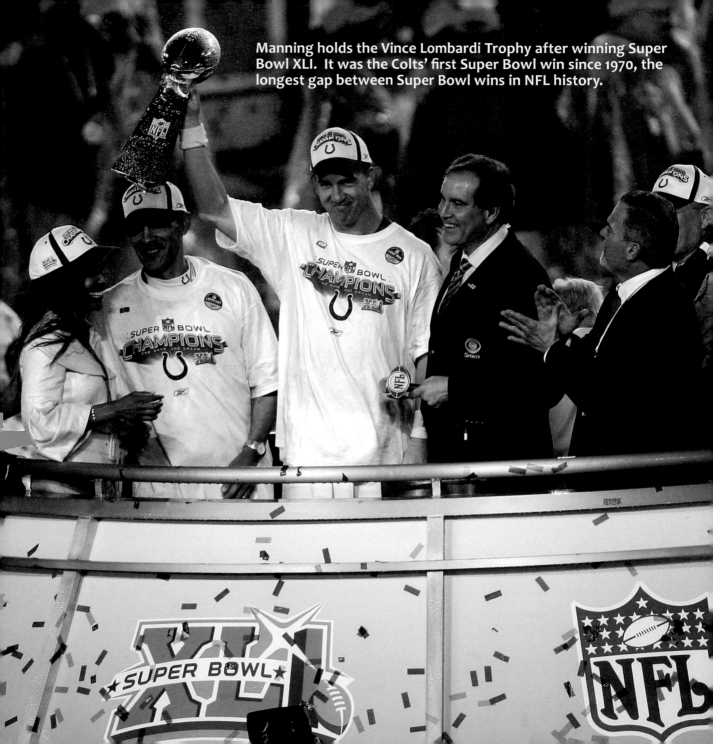

Manning holds the Vince Lombardi Trophy after winning Super Bowl XLI. It was the Colts' first Super Bowl win since 1970, the longest gap between Super Bowl wins in NFL history.

HIGHLIGHT REEL

Peyton Williams Manning was born in New Orleans, Louisiana.

1976

The Indianapolis Colts made Manning the first pick in the NFL Draft.

1998

Manning and the Colts lost to the New Orleans Saints in Super Bowl XLIV.

2010

Manning and the Broncos lost to the Seattle Seahawks in Super Bowl XLVIII.

2014

1994

Manning entered the University of Tennessee (UT). There, he set 42 college records and was a three-time Heisman Trophy candidate.

1999

Manning started the PeyBack Foundation.

2012

The Colts released Manning; he signed with the Denver Broncos.

1997

Manning graduated from UT with a degree in speech communications.

2007

Manning and the Colts beat the Chicago Bears in Super Bowl XLI.

PEYTON MANNING

DOB: March 24, 1976
Ht: 6'5"
Wt: 230
Position: QB
Number: 18

CAREER STATISTICS:

Passing Yards 64,694
Passing Touchdowns 491
Rushing Yards 697
Rushing Touchdowns 18
Quarterback Rating 115.1

AWARDS:

League MVP: 2003, 2004, 2008, 2009, 2013
Pro Bowl: 1999, 2000, 2002–2010, 2012, 2013
Super Bowl Champion: 2007
Super Bowl MVP: 2007

FOOTBALL FAMILY

Peyton Williams Manning was born on March 24, 1976, in New Orleans, Louisiana. He was Archie and Olivia Manning's second child. Peyton has an older brother, Cooper, and a younger brother, Eli.

Peyton's parents attended the University of Mississippi. His father was a record-breaking quarterback on the Rebels football team. When Peyton was born, his father was quarterback for the **NFL**'s New Orleans Saints.

Peyton learned at an early age to play catch with the football. By the time he was three years old, Peyton was playing with his brother Cooper.

In 1981, when Peyton was five, his brother Eli was born. The three boys were close. Like most brothers, they played together. Yet they also fought and sometimes teased one another!

However, homework came first in the Manning home. Sports came second. Peyton's parents wanted their boys to do well in school.

Eli, Archie, and Peyton Manning have all been NFL quarterbacks.

In 1983, Peyton's father was traded to the Minnesota Vikings. The Manning family moved between Minnesota and Louisiana over the following two years. So Peyton didn't begin playing youth league football until he was in seventh grade. But he had learned so much from his family that he **excelled** right away.

PREP STAR

In 1990, Peyton entered Isidore Newman High School in New Orleans. Cooper was a student there, too. Cooper was the quarterback on the Greenies football team.

Peyton wanted to play quarterback or defensive back. However, his skills developed quickly at quarterback. By the time he was a sophomore, Peyton was in control of the team's offense.

Cooper moved to wide receiver so that Peyton could quarterback the team. In the first game of the season, Peyton threw nine passes to Cooper in the first half alone! Together, Peyton and Cooper helped the Greenies to a 12–2 record.

The team advanced to the **playoffs**, but lost in the semifinal round. Peyton threw 23 touchdowns that year. Thirteen of them went to Cooper.

Peyton finished his high school career with a record of 34 wins and 5 losses. He passed for 7,207 yards (6,590 m) and 92 touchdowns. He was the country's top-rated **recruit**.

As a senior at Newman, Peyton was named the Gatorade Circle of Champions National Player of the Year.

COLLEGE DAYS

Many people thought that Peyton would attend the University of Mississippi. But he wanted a chance to be starting quarterback. So in 1994, Peyton entered the University of Tennessee (UT).

Peyton took over as starting quarterback early in his freshman season. He spent his first year learning how to be a leader on the field. Soon, Peyton's teammates trusted him. They knew that when he switched plays at the **line of scrimmage** it was because he saw things they did not. He could put his team in the best position to win.

And the Volunteers won a lot. Peyton was 39–6 as a starter for the Vols. He threw for 11,201 yards (10,242 m) and 89 touchdowns. He was a three-time candidate for the **Heisman Trophy**. He set 42 college records and was named a first team All-American. And in 1997, he graduated with a degree in speech communications.

On October 29, 2005, UT retired Peyton's No. 16 jersey.

DRAFT DAY

The 1998 **NFL Draft** was held on April 18 and 19. The Indianapolis Colts and the San Diego Chargers had the first two picks. Both teams needed a quarterback. Analysts believed Manning or Washington State University quarterback Ryan Leaf would be the first pick.

The Colts picked first and made Manning the draft's number one pick. The team's owners awarded him with a record-setting contract. Manning would earn $48 million. The contract made Manning the highest-paid NFL player in history.

The Colts had losing records for years leading up to Manning's arrival. Many in the NFL would joke about how many games the team lost. So, it didn't take long for head coach Jim Mora to make Manning the team's starting quarterback.

NUMBER ONE

MANNING'S FIRST NFL WIN WAS A 17–12 VICTORY OVER THE SAN DIEGO CHARGERS. HE COMPLETED 12 OF 23 PASSES FOR 137 YARDS (125 M). THE LOSING QUARTERBACK WAS RYAN LEAF, THE NUMBER TWO PICK AFTER MANNING IN THE DRAFT.

Of the eight quarterbacks picked in the 1998 NFL Draft, only Manning and Matt Hasselbeck are still in the league.

GIVING BACK

Manning's success gave him the means to help others. In 1999, he started the PeyBack Foundation. Through his foundation, Manning has raised thousands of dollars for **scholarships**, food banks, children's **literacy**, and healthy living programs.

In August 2005, Hurricane Katrina hit Louisiana, Mississippi, Alabama, and Florida. Manning thought of the people of New Orleans. He told reporters that they were like family to him. He had many friends there.

Manning and his brother Eli rented an airplane. They hired a crew and flew the plane to Indianapolis, Indiana. There, the brothers and volunteers loaded the plane with supplies to help storm victims.

Manning and his brother, New York Giants quarterback Eli (*center*), volunteered at a Red Cross shelter in Baton Rouge after Hurricane Katrina. There, Manning comforted a man who was searching for his missing sister.

In Louisiana, volunteers in Baton Rouge unloaded the plane. It contained 30,000 pounds (13,608 kg) of water, baby formula, Gatorade, and bedding. Those affected by the storm's devastation were comforted by these supplies and by the Manning family's support.

THE COLTS

During his **rookie** season, Manning threw for a record-breaking 3,379 yards (3,090 m) and 26 touchdowns. He set records for pass attempts and completions. Still, the Colts finished with a 3–13 record and missed the **playoffs**.

The Colts improved and made the playoffs each season from 2003 to 2005. Manning was named MVP in 2003 and 2004. Despite this success, the team could not reach the **Super Bowl**.

Finally, in 2006, the pieces came together. The Colts finished the regular season 12–4. They advanced to face the New England Patriots in the AFC Championship game.

The Colts were behind 21–6 at halftime. But Manning went on to complete 47 passes for 349 yards (319 m). The Colts won the game 38–34. For the first time since 1970, the Colts were going to the Super Bowl!

The Colts were down 18 points before Manning led his team to a 38–34 victory over the Patriots. It was the biggest comeback in conference title game history.

Manning's only interception in Super Bowl XLIV came in the fourth quarter. Tracy Porter made the pick and ran it back 74 yards (68 m) for a touchdown.

On a rainy day in Miami, Florida, the Colts beat the Chicago Bears to win **Super Bowl** XLI 29–17. Manning completed 25 passes for 247 yards (226 m). He was named the game's MVP.

The Colts' 2009 season looked to be historic. The team started 14–0. Manning threw for 4,500 yards (4,115 m) and 33 touchdowns. He won a league-record fourth MVP award.

The Colts took an **NFL**-best 14–2 record into the postseason. The team faced the Jets once again in the AFC Championship game. This time, the Colts were the victors with a 30–17 win behind Manning's 377-yard (345-m) passing performance. The win sent the Colts back to the Super Bowl.

On February 7, 2010, the Colts faced the New Orleans Saints in Super Bowl XLIV. The Colts led 10–6 at halftime. But it was not enough against a Saints team led by MVP quarterback Drew Brees. Brees completed a record-breaking 33 passes. Manning completed 31 passes for 333 yards (304 m), but the Saints defeated the Colts 31–17.

INJURED

The next season the Colts finished the regular season 10–6. The team made the **playoffs**, but did not advance in their division. They lost to the New York Jets 17–16.

Before the 2011 season began, the Colts announced that Manning would have surgery on his neck. On September 8, doctors worked to reconnect discs in Manning's spine. The surgery was successful. But Manning could not play during the 2011 season.

The Colts went 2–14 for the season. It was only the second season since Manning was a **rookie** that the Colts didn't win more than 10 games. The Colts' owner fired several managers and head coach Jim Caldwell. Manning's ability to play again was in doubt. So on March 7, 2012, the Colts released him.

Over 13 seasons, Manning led the Colts to eight division championships, two AFC championships, and a **Super Bowl** win. He threw for more than 54,828 yards

(50,135 m), completing more than 4,682 passes. He was a 4-time league MVP and 12-time **Pro Bowl** selection. It was tough for Manning to have been released by his team.

Manning leaves the field after completing 18 passes for 225 yards (206 m) and a touchdown against the Jets. It would be his final game as an Indianapolis Colt.

COMEBACK

Manning wasn't sure he wanted to play football anymore. He was worried he wouldn't be the same player he had been before his surgery. He talked it over with his wife, Ashley. She convinced him to give football another try.

Twelve teams had contacted Manning's **agents** after the Colts released him. One of them was the Denver Broncos. When the Broncos offered the job to Manning, he accepted. Manning signed with the Broncos on March 20, 2012.

Many people wondered how Manning would perform after his surgery. The answer was clear when Manning led the Broncos to the **playoffs** during his first season with the team. He provided the energy and **accurate** passing that the Broncos' offense needed.

In Manning's first season with the Broncos, he threw for 4,659 yards (4,260 m) and 37 touchdowns. He led the

FUN FACT

IN 2012, MANNING WAS NAMED THE ASSOCIATED PRESS NFL COMEBACK PLAYER OF THE YEAR.

team to a 13–3 record and the Broncos advanced to the **playoffs**. There, the Broncos lost to the Baltimore Ravens 38–35 in double **overtime**.

The playoff loss was disappointing to Broncos fans. But they were excited that Manning would lead the team again the next year.

Manning began his career with the Broncos by throwing his 400th touchdown pass in the season opener against the Pittsburgh Steelers.

STILL A STAR

In 2013, Manning led the Broncos to a 6–0 start. On October 20, the Broncos faced the Indianapolis Colts. It was the first time Manning had returned to Indy since his release. Fans gave Manning a warm welcome. But the Broncos lost to the Colts 39–33. The team would lose twice more to finish the regular season with a 13–3 record.

The Broncos met the New England Patriots in the AFC Championship game. Patriots quarterback Tom Brady completed 24 passes for 277 yards (253 m). But the Broncos, led by Manning's 32 completed passes for 400 yards (366 m), beat the Pats 26–16. The Broncos were headed to their first **Super Bowl** since 1998.

On February 2, 2014, the Broncos faced the Seattle Seahawks in Super Bowl XLVIII. The Seahawks had the **NFL**'s toughest defense. The Broncos had the top-scoring offense. Most football fans expected the Broncos to win.

But the Seahawks had figured out Manning's movements at the **line of scrimmage**. They began to guess which plays he would call by the hand signals he used. The Seahawks' swarming defense flushed Manning from the **pocket** and disrupted the Broncos' offense. The Seahawks won the game 43–8.

Though the Seahawks shut Manning down, he set a Super Bowl record with 34 completed passes.

LASTING LEGACY

After the **Super Bowl** loss to the Seahawks some people thought that Manning would retire. But Manning vowed to move forward. He expected that the loss would encourage the team to go all the way the next year.

In March 2014, Manning passed his physical exam. Right away he began working out with his teammates to prepare for the upcoming season.

Manning has left a lasting impact on the **NFL**. He is the league's only five-time MVP. Only Brett Favre has thrown more touchdown passes than Manning.

Peyton Manning has worked hard and remained focused on his goals. When the Denver Broncos begin their next season, don't be surprised if it ends with another trip to the Super Bowl!

Manning, shown here with his wife Ashley, was named *Sports Illustrated* **magazine's 2013 Sportsman of the Year.**

GLOSSARY

accurate - free from error.

agent - a person who represents another person in a business transaction.

draft - an event during which sports teams choose new players.

excel - to be better than others.

Heisman Trophy - an award given each year to the most outstanding player in college football.

line of scrimmage - a line across a football field based on the ball's location at the end of a play. Players may not cross the line until the next play begins.

literacy - the state of being able to read or write.

National Football League (NFL) - the highest level of professional football. It is made up of the American Football Conference (AFC) and the National Football Conference (NFC).

overtime - the extra time that is added to a game if the score is tied when the game clock runs out.

playoffs - a series of games that determine which team will win a championship.

pocket - an area in which the quarterback stands while the offense protects the player from the defense.

Pro Bowl - an all-star game in which the American Football Conference's top players play against the top players from the National Football Conference.

recruit - to get someone to join a group. A person who is recruited is called a recruit.

rookie - a first-year player in a professional sport.

scholarship - money or aid given to help a student continue his or her studies.

Super Bowl - the annual National Football League (NFL) championship game. It is played by the winners of the American and National Conferences.

WEBSITES

To learn more about Awesome Athletes, visit **booklinks.abdopublishing.com**. These links are routinely monitored and updated to provide the most current information available.

INDEX

A

AFC Championship (2006) 18, 22
AFC Championship (2009) 21, 22
AFC Championship (2013) 26
Alabama 16
awards 4, 12, 18, 21, 23, 28

B

birth 8
Brady, Tom 26
Brees, Drew 21

C

Caldwell, Jim 22
contract 14, 24

D

Denver Broncos 24, 25, 26, 27, 28

E

education 8, 9, 10, 12

F

family 8, 9, 10, 16, 17, 24
Favre, Brett 28
Florida 4, 16, 21

H

health 22, 24, 28
Hurricane Katrina 16, 17

I

Indiana 16, 26
Indianapolis Colts 4, 14, 18, 21, 22, 23, 24, 26

L

Leaf, Ryan 14
Louisiana 8, 9, 10, 16, 17

M

Minnesota 9
Mississippi 16
Mora, Jim 14

N

National Football League Draft 14

P

PeyBack Foundation 16
Pro Bowl 23

S

Super Bowl XLI 4, 18, 21, 22
Super Bowl XLIV 21
Super Bowl XLVIII 26, 27, 28

U

University of Mississippi 8, 12
University of Tennessee 12